The No-Bullying Program

Preventing Bully/Victim Violence at School

Program Director's Manual

James Bitney

Beverly B. Title, Ph.D.—Program Developer

JOHNSON INSTITUTE®

Minneapolis

Acknowledgment

The contents of this book are based on the No-Bullying Curriculum model originally developed for the St. Vrain Valley School District, Longmont, Colorado, by Beverly B. Title, with assistance from Lisa Anderson-Goebel, Vivian Bray, K.G. Campanella-Green, Ted Goodwin, Karen Greene, Elizabeth Martinson, Mike O'Connell, and Peggy Stortz.

The Bullying Behavior Chart was developed by Beverly B. Title, Ph.D.; Severance Kelly, M.D.; Louis Krupnik, Ph.D.; Joseph Matthews, M.S.W.; Kendra Bartley, M.A.

Curriculum consultation was provided by Peggy O'Connell.

The No-Bullying Program: Preventing Bully/Victim Violence at School

Program Director's Manual by James Bitney
Beverly B. Title, Ph.D., Program Developer

Johnson Institute
7205 Ohms Lane
Minneapolis, Minnesota 55439-2159
612-831-1630 or 800-231-5165

ISBN 1-56246-114-1

Logo design: Diana Garcia
Cover and text design: Crombie Design
Artwork by Sally Brewer Lawrence
Printed in the United States of America
96 97 98 99 / 5 4 3 2 1

Contents

Introduction

Imagine a scenario like the following:

> A lawyer stands before the Supreme Court representing a class action suit brought by the children of the United States. The lawyer argues that mandating school attendance constitutes cruel and unusual punishment in violation of the Eighth Amendment of the Constitution of the United States. In support of the case, the lawyer has filed numerous briefs, each listing thousands—literally thousands—of instances of cruelty, harassment, abuse, and other forms of violence perpetrated upon clients by peers in the U.S. school system. The briefs also include documented evidence of the nation's school systems' efforts—mostly failed efforts—to deal with such cruelty. The lawyer argues that schools must offer children education not victimization, and that no one should be mandated to endure an environment teeming with violence and rife with fear.

Does such a scene seem too far-fetched? Maybe so. Maybe no. Statistics reveal that violence in schools is widespread and growing. A 1993 survey of 65,000 students indicated the following:

- 37% of students do not feel safe in school (nearly double the number compared to a similar survey taken in 1989).

- 20% avoid hallways.

- 43% avoid school rest rooms.

- 45% avoid school grounds.

- 26% of the girls and 49% of the boys reported being physically assaulted.

- 50% knew of a student who switched schools to feel safer.

- 22% of students say that an item worth more than $10 has been stolen from them.

- 79% of students say that violence is often precipitated by "stupid things like bumping into someone."

- Every school day, 160,000 students avoid going to certain classes because they fear being harmed physically.

- 20,000 students are attacked physically at school every day.

- 20% of the students carry weapons to school on a regular basis.

- 63% of the students say that they would learn more if they felt safer in school.

- 81% of the students say that they would be happier if they felt safer at school.

Teachers do not fare much better. A report from the National Education Association indicates that every month of the school year 12% of teachers will have something stolen, 6,000 will have something taken from them forcefully, 120,000 will be threatened, 5,200 will be attacked, and 19% of those attacked will require medical attention.

Statistics are one thing. First-hand reports are another. In late 1995, in a monthly forum for young readers called "Mindworks," the Minneapolis, Minnesota daily newspaper, *StarTribune*, asked young readers to respond to this question:

> "Have you or anyone you know ever been teased, bullied, or harassed? Have you ever teased, bullied, or harassed anyone? Why do children and teens behave this way? What can teachers and other adults do to help?"

The first-hand reports the newspaper received revealed the fear and hurt experienced by the victims of violent behavior:

> "When I get teased it makes me feel sad. Sometimes I feel like I'm in a world with only bullies and no friends." (a rural sixth grader)

> "I've been bullied before and it isn't fun. My knees were shaking and it was scary, like you just want to cry for your mommy or put (the bully) in jail." (an urban third grader)

"Adults just don't seem to understand what it feels like to be teased. If they
did, they wouldn't act like it's okay. When somebody teases you, it feels
like they just punched you in the stomach." (a suburban fifth grader)

The newspaper received over 12,000 such responses from students of all ages,
both urban and rural—12,000! Their first-hand accounts point out that many see
school as little more than a daily gauntlet of violence that they are forced to run.

Violence is happening in our schools. It happens on the school bus that
primary children ride. It happens on the playground where elementary children play. It happens in the lunchroom where all children eat. It happens in
the lavatories when teachers are not present. It happens in the hallways where
middle school students move from class to class. And it happens in the classroom where teachers are trying to teach and students are trying to learn.

What's to be done? Perhaps the best answer comes from an eleven-year-
old girl who writes:

"Teachers and other adults need to teach kids that violence is not the
answer for anything and that we all need help sometimes so we aren't so
violent. Everyone deserves a great childhood without violence."

Chapter 1: Creating a Great Childhood Without Violence

To help create a great childhood without violence, it seems crucial, first of all, to agree on just what violence is. Unfortunately, violence means different things to different people. It is a diffuse problem, appearing in many different forms and with many different interpretations. As educators, we need a clear definition of violence in order to set boundaries and to leave no room for ambivalence or individual interpretation of violent behaviors and incidents. Once defined, we can use the definition as a tool for intervention and prevention and for clarifying for our students what behaviors are unacceptable.

The Johnson Institute suggests the following simple definition of violence for educators:

> **Any word, look, sign, or act that inflicts or threatens to inflict physical or emotional injury or discomfort upon another person's body, feelings, or possessions.**

The above definition is purposefully broad. It deliberately includes what may appear to be fairly "normal" or "innocent" behaviors like joking or teasing. It does so because it recognizes the potential such behaviors have for causing real emotional and physical harm.

Included within this broad definition of violence are two important delineations or types of violence: peer violence and bully/victim violence.

- **Peer violence** is defined as acts of violence stemming from disagreements, misunderstandings, or conflicting desires among students who are equally matched in strength and power.

- **Bully/victim** violence involves an imbalance of power and strength between students; bully/victim violence occurs whenever a student *intentionally, repeatedly, and over time* inflicts or threatens to inflict physical or emotional injury or discomfort on another's body, feelings, or possessions.

Both types of violence must be dealt with to make our schools safe and violence-free.

Schools have and continue to deal successfully with the problem of peer violence by helping students grow in social skills:

- communication

- feeling processing

- problem solving

- conflict management

- conflict mediation

Utilizing these techniques in attempting to stem bully/victim violence, however, has not proved successful. Why not?

Research has clearly shown that those who bully do not respond to social skill work. They do not care that what they are doing is creating problems for others. In fact, they generally enjoy the results of their bullying behavior. What schools need is a research-based, educational model to deal with bully/victim violence in the school, to help schools become violence-free, and thus, to create for our children "a great childhood without violence...." The *No-Bullying Program* has been developed to meet that need.

Chapter 2: Research On Bully/ Victim Violence

The school-yard bully is a common theme in human experience, often appearing in literature and movies. Until recently, however, bullying has been greatly misunderstood, and we, as adults, are generally misguided in the advice that we give to children with regard to dealing with bullying. Happily, however, recent research offers new information and a basis for much improved strategies to address bully/victim violence.

Dan Olweus from the University of Bergen in Norway has been publishing on the topic of bully/victim violence since 1972. Considered the "founding father" of research on problems of bullying and victimization, Olweus has conducted studies that elucidate some characteristics of bully/victim violence, distinguish it from peer violence or normal peer conflict, and discredit much of the folklore about those who engage in bullying behavior.[1]

Based on his research, Olweus says:

"A person is being bullied when he or she is exposed, repeatedly and over time, to negative actions on the part of one or more persons."[2]

Bullying behavior can be described under three headings:

• Physical Bullying: harm to another's body or property

• Emotional Bullying: harm to another's self-esteem

---

[1] In addition to Olweus' studies in Norway, research on bullying is also being reported from many other parts of the world: England (M.J. Bolton, P.K. Smith, and D. Thompson); China (S. Ekblad and D. Olweus); United States (D. Farrington); Sweden (P.P. Heinemann); Japan (K. Hirano); the Netherlands (M. Junger); Ireland (M. O'More and H. Brendan); Australia (K. Rigby and P. Slee); Spain (R.O. Ruiz; Canada (S. Ziegler and M. Rosenstein-Manner).

[2] Dan Olweus, Ph.D. 1991. "Bully/Victim Problems Among Schoolchildren: Basic Facts and Effects of a School Based Intervention Program," Debra J. Pepler and Kenneth H. Rubin, eds. *The Development and Treatment of Childhood Aggression*. Hillsdale, NJ: Lawrence Erlbaum Associates, Publishers, 413.

- Social Bullying: harm to another's group acceptance

Bullying behavior may also be verbal or non-verbal and range along a continuum of less to more severe. For example, verbal bullying may extend from teasing all the way to extortion or death threats. Non-verbal bullying may extend from giving dirty looks to ostracizing.

Imbalance of power is the primary quality that characterizes bullying. That imbalance might be due to superior physical strength, but it also might issue from superior intelligence (for example, "street smarts") or might issue from sources such as economics, ethnicity, social skill, weapons, information, and so on. Those who engage in bullying behavior take unfair advantage of a weaker party.

Bullying is also more than a single act. It is a pattern of behavior. Those who bully repeatedly engage in conflicts that they are sure to win due to their superior power, and they are merciless in their tactics.[3]

Bullying is a function of a dynamic relationship involving an imbalance of power and repetition. No matter the type of bullying behavior, bullying always involves the repeated exploitation of a person with less power by a person with greater power. The seriousness of all levels and all types of bullying behavior, therefore, must be evaluated based upon the harm to the victim and the frequency of the occurrences.

---

[3] "Bullies need to assert their power by subduing their victims, and show little empathy for their victims. They are usually very defiant and aggressive toward adults (including teachers and parents), often frightening them. Moreover, they are skilled at intimidating other students, as well as inducing them to become followers." Dan Olweus, Ph.D. 1993. *Bullying at School: What We Know and What We Can Do.* Cambridge, Mass.: Blackwell Publishers, 59.

Chapter 3: Bullies and Their Victims

Who Are the Bullies?

Research has shown that many of the behaviors and characteristics customarily associated with bullies and their victims are merely stereotypes and are generally untrue. If adults base their work with children on such stereotypes, they will mismanage the problem of bully/victim violence. To avoid that eventuality, let's take a look at some of the myths surrounding bullying.

Debunking the Myths

Only boys bully. Both males and females may engage in bullying behavior. However, different genders tend to use different methods of bullying: males, physical and verbal aggression; females, social alienation and both overt and subtle intimidation.

Once a bully, always a bully. Bullying behavior is learned; as such, it can be unlearned. Like any other behavior, the sooner change is begun, the better, and the easier it is to accomplish. Likewise, those who bully require motivation to change.

Those who bully have low self-esteem. Those who bully often have very high self-esteem; their superior power is a source of great personal pride.

Bullies are only from poor families. Bullying occurs at all socioeconomic levels.

All bullying involves physical aggression. Although the misuse of physical force is a favorite and common tactic of those who bully, many use other methods to enforce their dominance over a victim (e.g., social alienation or advanced verbal ability).

Bullies generally do poorly in school. Those who bully are most often average students.

Bullies are agitated and aggressive. When confronted about their bullying behaviors, most children who bully tend to maintain an even emotional tone, even a flat affect. Typically, it is the victim of a bully who is upset and distressed: tearful, angry, fearful.

Most bullying happens away from (on the way to or on the way from) school. Most bullying happens at school.

Ending bullying at school means that bullying will just continue out of school. Research has found that bullying can be interrupted both in and out of school. A school's no-tolerance toward bullying tends to "spread."

Standing up to a bully (fighting back) will deter his or her bullying. This is probably the most dangerous myth surrounding bullying. Those who bully are excited by the victim who fights back. Fighting back may prompt a bully to even more severe bullying.

Characteristics of Those Who Bully

The following traits are characteristic of those who bully:

- Most children who bully have a significant role model (parent, older sibling, older friend) who models aggressive or violent behavior.

- Those who bully are excited by their bullying behavior.

- Whether boys or girls, children who engage in bullying behavior enjoy being in charge, in control. They want to be "winners" and tend to assert their positions with power.

- Since those who bully dominate others, they, in fact, do tend to "win" over others and soon come to value the rewards bullying affords.

- They look upon those who are their victims with little or no empathy or compassion, believing that their victims have provoked aggression (blaming the victim) and deserve what they get.

- Those who bully usually feel no guilt for their behavior and tend to think unrealistically (for example, "I should always have my own way" or "Anyone who disagrees with me is out to get me.")

- Children who bully are usually average students who are neither anxious nor insecure, and who have fairly high self-esteem.

- Children who bully are not loners; they usually have a small, tight network of friends.

- Children who bully are very successful at hiding their behavior from adults.

- Children who bully are excited by the reaction of a victim, whether the reaction is fear, crying, or fighting back.

- Children who bully feel comfortable with and justified in their behavior.

Bullying Behaviors

Studies have shown that bullying behaviors include not only forms of physical aggression, but also emotional harassment, social alienation, and both subtle and overt intimidation (the latter often being—but not exclusively—the behavior of girls who engage in bullying). No matter the type, bullying behaviors are usually difficult to detect, and yet, studies also indicate that all types of bullying occur at school.

The following "Bullying Behavior Chart" details many of the tactics or behaviors of those who bully. In viewing the chart, note the range and scope of behaviors. Note, too, that since these behaviors are *learned*, they can be *unlearned*.

Bullying Behavior Chart

LEVELS	Physical — Harm to another's body or property		Emotional — Harm to another's self-esteem		Social — Harm to another's group acceptance	
	verbal	non-verbal	verbal	non-verbal	verbal	non-verbal
1	Taunting Expressing physical superiority	Making threatening gestures Defacing property Pushing/shoving Taking small items from others	Insulting remarks Calling names Teasing about possessions, clothes	Giving dirty looks Holding nose or other insulting gestures Saying someone has germs or is unclean	Gossiping Starting/spreading rumors Teasing publicly about clothes, looks, etc…	Passively not including in group Playing mean tricks
2	Threatening physical harm Blaming victim	Damaging property Stealing Initiating fights Scratching Tripping or causing a fall Assaulting	Insulting family Harassing with phone calls Insulting intelligence, athletic ability, etc…	Defacing school work Falsifying school work Defacing personal property, clothing, etc…	Insulting race, gender Increasing gossip/rumors Undermining other relationships	Making someone look foolish Excluding from the group
3	Making repeated and/or graphic threats Practicing extortion Making threats to secure silence: "If you tell, I will…"	Destroying property Setting fires Biting Physical cruelty Making repeated, violent threats Assaulting with a weapon	Frightening with phone calls Challenging in public	Ostracizing Destroying personal property or clothing	Threatening total group exclusion	Arranging public humiliation Total group rejection/ostracizing

Who Are the Victims?

The classic image of the victim of bullying as a "wimp" just does not wash. Research has revealed that there are two types of victims: passive victims and provocative victims. There is a great deal of difference between the two types. In fact, provocative victims are easily mistaken for bullies, because they tend to be very aggressive. Nevertheless, both types end up on the "losing" end in a bullying situation.

Characteristics of Both Types of Victims

Both passive and provocative victims:

- are very emotional and have a lot of affect
- rarely report being bullied, because they fear it will only make matters worse
- do not believe that adults can help
- sometimes carry weapons to protect themselves from bullying

Characteristics of Passive Victims

Passive victims of bullying:

- do not invite attack
- are sensitive
- generally lack social skills
- usually are lacking in humor
- are loners, friendless, the last to be chosen to join with others
- feel isolated
- depend on adults
- are anxious and distressed
- can be learning disabled
- may have a physical or mental disability
- are repeatedly bullied

- may have experienced a past trauma such as rape, abuse, incest

- are bullied by someone much stronger, larger, or more powerful

- may try to use bribes (money, toys, favors) to protect themselves

- are shy

- are often small for their age

- are insecure

Characteristics of Provocative Victims

Provocative victims of bullying:

- repeatedly pester and irritate others

- are quick-tempered and will fight back

- get others charged up

- may be diagnosed with ADHD (Attention Deficit Hyperactive Disorder)

- may be clumsy, immature, restless

- provoke attack

- may look as if they are bullies, because they tend to maintain the conflict; however, unlike bullies, they always lose in the end.

A Victim Is a Victim Is a Victim

Victims of bullying, whether passive or provocative, share a common denominator. They are victims. The bullying is not their fault. Victimized children rarely tell others of their plight. As a result, they live in fear and suffer in silence. They are on the losing end of a downward spiral, the effects of which may last throughout their lives. Victims need and deserve our help.

Chapter 4: The No-Bullying Program: A System-Wide Approach To Ending Bullying In School

When bullying exists in a school, the problem extends beyond those who bully and those who are bullied. Bullying in a school is a systemic problem. Approximately 15% of any school population are bullies or victims of bullies, which means that 85% of the school population are relatively uninvolved in bullying behaviors. This does not mean, however, that the 85% are not affected. Bully/victim violence has a "spreading effect." If a school tolerates bullying, soon everyone becomes a victim, for tolerance leads to entitlement; those who engage in bullying feel that they are "entitled" to continue such behavior. Moreover, tolerating bullying often incites other students, who might not otherwise act in violent ways, to become violent because they perceive tolerance as *permission* to become violent.

The No-Bullying Program takes a system-wide approach to ending bullying in school. It involves all school personnel, students, parents, and concerned community members. Thus, it is both adult-centered and student-centered.

*For adults, **The No-Bullying Program*** seeks the support and involvement of all school personnel (administration, teachers, support staff). It asks that all adults agree both that students have a right to feel safe in their schools and that adults have a responsibility to secure that safety. Research and experience both have shown that adult-centered action with regard to eliminating bullying is crucial and that it works.

*For students, **The No-Bullying Program*** consists of two components:

- a prevention component
- an intervention component

The prevention component consists of curricula designed to engage the help of the 85% of students who are not directly involved in bullying behaviors (either as bullies or as victims) by helping them:

- define and understand what is and what is not bullying

- better understand bullying and its effects

- develop empathy for the victims of bullying

- learn when and how to report bullying

- discover the school's consequences for engaging in bullying behavior

The curricula provide classroom session plans and materials for students in the following four grade levels:

- Kindergarten and First Grade

- Second and Third Grade

- Fourth and Fifth Grade

- Middle School

The intervention component includes swift, severe, and consistent responses (consequences) to those who engage in bullying behaviors; these responses—although non-hostile and non-physical—are strictly imposed and enforced by adults in the school.

> **Note:** that *The No-Bullying Program* is not based on retribution. Its aim is not to punish students who engage in bullying. Rather, its primary objective is to shift the balance of power away from those who bully by empowering other students and adults in the school to confront them with their unacceptable behaviors. Its secondary objective is to allow those who bully to experience the consequences of those behaviors.[4] *The No-Bullying Program* takes pains never to label a stu-

---

[4] Although those students who engage in bullying behaviors comprise only about 15% of the school population, they have a huge impact on our resources. Likewise, research has shown that the majority of those who bully become incarcerated by their mid-twenties; many have multiple felony convictions (Olweus, 1991, p. 425); and their victims often display depressive tendencies and poor self-esteem as adults, and thus deplete social services (Olweus, "Victimization by Peers," 1993, p. 331). Allowing those who engage in bullying to experience the consequences of their behavior, therefore, can pay great dividends not only in the present, but in the future as well.

dent a "bully." Bullying is a learned behavior and thus can be changed. In seeking to interrupt and re-direct bullying behaviors *The No-Bullying Program* is seeking to help both the victims of bullying and it perpetrators.

When students see adults united in action against bullying—when they see that adults will not tolerate it—they will follow such positive leadership and will feel empowered to join with school personnel to help monitor their school and keep it safe and free of bullying.

An important part of the school-wide approach includes using the tools of public relations and marketing to get students to buy into the program. The program logo can be used to heighten program visibility. Posters of the logo should be placed in each classroom, the halls, cafeteria, the administative office, counseling office, and any other appropriate places. These give a strong visual message that reminds students about the program and your expectations of their behavior.

Each adult in the school should have a No-Bullying Tee shirt. The shirts should be worn to the Kick-Off Assembly and during the introduction of the program. Some playground supervisors have several shirts, because they like to wear them frequently. They report that they can just point to their shirts and see a behavior shift among a group of students, without having to say a word. Also, a good follow-up activity is for all the staff to wear their shirts to school on the same day. This can be an effective reminder about behavior expectations, again, without a word being spoken. Some schools have done this on the day before a holiday break when student behavior is often less controlled.

PROTOTYPE

Chapter 5: Implementing The No-Bullying Program in Your School

To assure the success of *The No-Bullying Program*, *everyone* in the school must understand and agree that bullying behavior will not be tolerated. Both adults (school staff) and students must commit themselves to intervene in bullying behavior when they spot it. To this end, you will need to take the following steps:

1. Create a Strategy Statement

2. Gain Administrative Support/"Principal" Participation

3. Secure Parental Support

4. Involve the Broader Community

5. Establish Consequences for Bullying (that are consistently administered)

6. Train School Staff (especially those who will deliver the curricula)

Creating a Strategy Statement

The first step in helping your school population unite against bullying is developing a comprehensive strategy statement regarding bullying in the school. Happily—if we may use that word—bullying in a school is different from other systemic problems. Fear of bullying motivates most students and staff to do something about it. They simply need to be shown how much power they have to transform their school into a safe environment. A comprehensive strategy statement regarding bullying should include the following elements:

- A definition of violence: *Any word, look, sign, or act that inflicts or threatens to inflict physical or emotional injury or discomfort upon another person's body, feelings, or possessions.*

- A definition of bullying: *Bullying occurs whenever a student intentionally, repeatedly, and over time inflicts or threatens to inflict physical or emotional injury or discomfort on another's body, feelings, or possessions.*

- A clear assertion of no-tolerance/no-entitlement regarding bullying: *Bullying is not allowed. Staff will intervene in bullying and strictly enforce rules against bullying.*

- A simple declaration of student responsibility: *Students will report bullying behavior and treat one another with respect.*

Thus, a school's comprehensive strategy statement may look something like the following:

We recognize violence as any word, look, sign, or act that inflicts or threatens to inflict physical or emotional injury or discomfort upon another person's body, feelings, or possessions. We also recognize bullying as a type of violence that occurs whenever a student intentionally, repeatedly, and over time inflicts or threatens to inflict physical or emotional injury or discomfort on another's body, feelings, or possessions. To make our school violence-free and safe from bullying, we pledge to:

- *tolerate no bullying in our school*

- *intervene in bullying behaviors and strictly enforce rules against bullying*

- *empower students to report bullying behavior and to treat one another with respect*

Such a statement makes it clear to everyone involved—school staff, students, and parents—that your school is not only committed to ending bullying, but also what that commitment involves.

Gaining Administrative Support/"Principal" Participation

Since one of the startling research findings about the victims of bullying is that they do not believe that adults can help them with their problem, *The No-Bullying Program* relies on the "hands-on" participation of the school principal (or other administrator) to counteract this belief. Past experience has taught too many students that the conventional wisdom among adults is that "children have to learn to solve their own problems." Such "wisdom," however, is not so wise when applied to bully/victim conflict.

Students need powerful reassurance that those in positions of authority in the school will not allow bullying to continue once they are made aware of it. Thus, *The No-Bullying Program requires* the school principal to visit classrooms to give students his or her personal guarantee about how their reports of bullying will be received and what will be done about them. Students need to hear and believe that adults in the school now know more about bullying than they did in the past and that they are committed to ending it and to protecting those who are its victims.

Securing Parental Support

Prior to presenting *The No-Bullying Program* curricula to students, parents should be informed of its implementation. Once established, parents need to know the formal school strategy or policy regarding bullying and be made aware of both the prevention and intervention (consequences) components of the program. Parents need information both on how to report to school staff (for example, a specific contact person) if they believe their child is being bullied and on what will take place if their child is engaging in bullying. At the same time, they need solid guarantees that no child will be labeled as either a bully or a victim.

Send a letter to all parents informing them of your school's plans regarding *The No-Bullying Program* (see the "Sample Letter to Parents" in the Appendix, page 36 of this manual). In the letter, tell parents about the school's policy regarding bullying and the strategy statement regarding ending bullying in the school. Invite parents to attend a meeting at which the program will be more fully explained.

The No-Bullying Program: A Guide for Families is a pamphlet that explains the program. We recommend that you send a copy of this pamphlet to every family in your school. These are available from the Johnson Institute.

Schedule an orientation meeting or workshop for parents to inform and educate them about bullying. Help them recognize what they can do about bullying. For example:

- Know where their child is, whom he or she is with, and what he or she is doing.

- Monitor such things as their child's TV viewing and video game playing, much of which promotes aggression as the only way to resolve conflicts.

- Ask their child how peers treat them; believing that adults can do little about the problem, most children are afraid or embarrassed to bring up to adults—even to parents—the fact that they are being bullied.

- Allow—encourage—their child to develop skills that are valued by their peers (e.g., sports, musicianship, etc.).

- Apply fair, timely, and appropriate discipline.

- Help their child expand their social circle by welcoming their friends to your home; get to know their child's peers and their parents.

- Know what's going on in—and participate in—their child's life.

- Emphasize the positive to raise their child's self-esteem and self-confidence; praise, encourage, and approve of their child.

- Help their child resolve conflicts and solve problems at home.

- Promote goal setting.

In addition to the orientation meeting, use natural contact with parents to inform them of the school's no-bullying policy. This can occur at PTA meetings, during parent conferences, on report card day, or through a mailing sent to all parents. The pamphlet mentioned earlier can do much to educate parents and convince them that the no-bullying program is important.

During the meeting, draw on information in this manual to outline behaviors that indicate to parents that their child might be either engaging in bullying behavior or a victim of bullying. Stress to parents that contrary to popular belief, engaging in bullying or being a victim of same, is not "just a part of growing up." Emphasize that dealing effectively with bullying almost always involves adult intervention. Depending on the consequences for engaging in bullying set by your school (see pages 24–25 of this manual), make it clear to parents how the school will deal with episodes of bullying (both for those who bully and its victims) and how parents will be involved.

Offer or support offerings of parent-training classes that teach sound parenting skills; for example, how to use natural and logical consequences with children; training in the skills parents need to help their children grow in self-esteem; encouragement to help parents instill empathy in their children for those who are the victims of bullying.

Remember that although all parents want school to be safe for their children, not all parents will readily support efforts at ending bullying. The myth that bullying is simply a rite of passage, a passing stage, is pervasive in our society,[5] and aggression is often confused with self-assertiveness. (See Chapter 7: "Family Matters," pages 27–28 of this manual, for more on dealing with the parents of children involved in bullying.)

Involving the Broader Community

Create support networks with community leaders and service providers, professionals in the areas of violence and domestic abuse, law enforcement officials, and parent advisory group leaders or members. Keep the above informed regarding your efforts at implementing *The No-Bullying Program*. Encourage school participation in community service programs that help students take "ownership" of their community and grow in personal self-worth and self-respect.

Establishing Consequences for Bullying

It is imperative that the entire school staff be involved in setting and committing themselves to the consistent enforcement of school-wide consequences for those who engage in bullying behaviors. There can be no inconsistency in communication and demonstration of consequences, or students will conclude that some adults sanction bullying and that it is acceptable. The consequences should be of a non-physical, non-hostile nature, and understandable to the students. Chapter 6 contains specific levels of consequences that can be used by your school, although they may be adapted to fit your particular school's needs.

Training School Staff

Everyone and anyone who supervises students anywhere in the school needs to be involved in training, not simply those who will deliver *The No-Bullying Program* curricula. Although this manual does not purport to be a training guide, the following chapter will outline procedures you may choose to follow as you train school staff in the principles of *The No-Bullying Program*.

---

[5] Bullying is, in fact, anything but a passing stage. Once again, research has shown that those who bully as children continue to do so as adults. They continue to engage in behavior that impedes learning, destroys relationships, influences earning ability, and deteriorates mental health.

Chapter 6: Staff Training

Before presenting *The No-Bullying Program* curricula and involving the students, consider the following seven-step plan of staff training:

1. Present and gain consensus on the school-wide strategy statement regarding bullying in the school.

2. Overview *The No-Bullying Program's* information about bullying: its perpetrators and its victims.

3. Help school staff discover how "enabling" fosters bullying behavior.

4. Establish a procedure to help students feel safe when reporting bullying.

5. Set and commit to the consistent enforcement of school-wide consequences for those engaging in bullying behaviors.

6. Identify those who will deliver the curricula to the students and review the material in the manuals.

7. Decide how to measure the effectiveness of the program.

Step 1

Present and gain consensus on the school-wide strategy statement regarding bullying in the school. Once you have developed a strategy statement (see page 16), present and explain it to school staff—giving everyone a copy. It's essential that staff understand the statement and feel comfortable with it in order to back it up when applying it to bullying situations.

Step 2

Present an overview of The *No-Bullying Program's* information about bullying: its pepetrators and its victims. Drawing on the material contained in

Chapters 2 and 3 of this manual, create a presentation that examines the research on bullying, corrects misinformation about it, and describes its perpetrators and its victims. Take time to explain that the difference between programs dealing with conflict resolution or peer mediation and *The No-Bullying Program* is that adults need to take more proactive roles when dealing with bullies and their victims. Bullying cannot be fixed by teaching social skills or by having the parties talk it over. Adults must intervene to end bullying.

Step 3

Help school staff discover how "enabling" fosters bullying behavior. Help staff recognize that tolerance and entitlement toward bullying in a school are fostered by an enabling system of which they are a part. That enabling system is made up of all the misguided beliefs, feelings, attitudes, and behaviors that unwittingly allow and encourage bullying to continue or worsen by preventing those who engage in bullying from understanding and experiencing the consequences of their behavior. Enabling may be good intentions, but it is also bad results.[6]

Make copies of the "Enabling Checklist" on pages 34–35 of this manual. Ask staff to complete the list to help them discover whether they are harboring any misguided beliefs, feelings, attitudes, or behaviors that may be enabling bullying in your school.

To interpret the checklist, ask staff to count the number of statements they checked "Sometimes." Then, explain:

- Checking "Sometimes" for *any* statement means that the belief, feeling, attitude, or behavior described in the statement may be an enabling problem for you.

- Checking "Sometimes" for more than four statements means that you are involved in a pattern of enabling that negatively impacts your relationships.

- A response of "Sometimes" to any statement may indicate involvement in enabling a student who is engaging in bullying behavior.

Be sure to emphasize to staff that enabling doesn't *cause* bullying, because enabling is unwitting and unintentional. That is, school staff are *not responsible for bullying* in their school. However, school staff are responsible to stop

---

[6] For a more thorough examination of enabling, see Remboldt, Carole. *Violence in Schools: The Enabling Factor.* Minneapolis: Johnson Institute-QVS, Inc., 1994.

enabling and to allow those who *are responsible for bullying*—those who engage in bullying behaviors—to face the consequences.

Step 4

Establish a procedure to help students feel safe when reporting bullying.
One of the major thrusts of *The No-Bullying Program* curricula is convincing students of their responsibility to report bullying and when and how to report it. To enable students to feel safe when reporting bullying, your school staff needs to establish a reporting procedure for students to follow.

Given that bullying has so long been enabled in our schools, it should come as no surprise that students are unwilling to get involved in dealing with bullying when they see it happening to another. Many students believe that telling adults about bullying will only make matters worse. In fact, that perception may well be the students' experience with bully/victim conflict, especially given the far too pervasive climate of tolerance and entitlement that has long surrounded bullying.

From early training, children—even the most caring—have been advised not to tell on others and to deal with conflicts on their own. This is good advice when the conflict is between individuals equal in power. However, it is not good counsel in a bully/victim situation, because, as we have clearly seen, the victim can never win. Thinking that a victim of bullying can resolve the problem on his or her own without help is like thinking a child can solve a problem in quantum physics without help.

Victims of, and, often, witnesses to bullying are afraid to report it. They fear both physical retribution and social ostracism. Students need to feel secure that all school staff are committed to protecting the victims of bullying—both from further bullying and from retribution for reporting such behavior—and that students reported for bullying will be watched, dealt with appropriately, and held strictly accountable for any subsequent bullying behavior.

As a staff, you need to establish a procedure for students to report bullying. That procedure should make clear:

- how students are to report

- to whom they are to report

- when and where they are to report

- the school's guarantee of anonymity to the reporter

Those who will be delivering *The No-Bullying Program* curricula will need to have this procedure in place before presenting it to their students, all of whom must be able to understand it and access it. If your school has a Student Assistance Program (SAP), you may wish to call on its director to offer assistance in designing this important process.

There should be one person who collects all reports of bullying in the school. Bullying is likely to occur at any number of locations and a variety of staff may see it or get reports from students. Therefore, one person needs to receive the reports and, if possible, log them on a computer data base. That way a report can be called up by name of student who is bullying, name of student who is victimized, location of bullying, etc. On a weekly basis, a person (or a committee including administration, counseling staff, etc.) should review the reports. They should look for any patterns of behavior that may be seen. Additionally, they may determine if consequences need to be given and at what level. Without a central collection and review, lots of bullying can fall through the cracks.

Step 5

Set and commit to the consistent enforcement of school-wide consequences for those engaging in bullying behaviors. Involve the entire school staff in setting and in committing themselves to the consistent enforcement of school-wide consequences for those who engage in bullying behaviors.

Staff need input on, and need to agree on, clear expectations of student behavior and consequences for bullying in the school. If school staff do not consistently communicate and demonstrate that there are consequences for bullying, then students will feel free to—and, indeed, will—conclude that adults sanction bullying and that it is, therefore, acceptable.

With staff, establish clear, enforceable consequences for bullying in your school. The consequences themselves should be non-physical and non-hostile responses to bullying that are consistent throughout the school.

The final session of each of the four levels of The **No-Bullying Program** curriculum involves the school principal in personally presenting these consequences to the children. Thus, as with the procedure for reporting bullying, remember to make the consequences for engaging in bullying understandable to the students.

The *No-Bullying Program* suggests the following three levels of consequences,[7] each of which is progressively more severe:

Consequences

Level 1: Verbal Discussion—Parents Notified

Level 2: Denial of Activity Where Bullying Behavior Occurred

Level 3: Time Out (Detention) and Development of an Individual Behavior Plan

The behavior plan may include the following escalating options:

A. Suspension or Therapy Group Option

B. Suspension Extended **or** Parent Volunteer Assigned to Accompany Student Throughout the School Day

C. Expulsion Proceedings

The No-Bullying Program does not prescribe that your school use the above consequences. However, prior to curricula delivery, it is absolutely imperative that your school staff establish appropriate consequences that can he adhered to on a school-wide basis.

The procudeures for your school will need to be in alignment with your local board of education and your state laws related to suspension and expulsion.

It is important to have some activities in place to assist both the students who are bullying and those who have been bullied. We urge you to get counseling staff to offer support groups in anger management for bullying students and assertiveness for stduents who are bullied.

Step 6

Identify those who will deliver the curricula to the students and review the material in the manuals. Since, in most cases, it is advisable that regular classroom teachers deliver the curricula to the students, extensive training in class-

---

[7] When ground-breaking no-bullying programs were developed in Norway, the consequences for engaging in bullying behavior were set for three levels, with each level being progressively more severe. By the time a student had reached the third level, he or she was not allowed to return to school. The bullying student could enroll in another school in the district, but not back in the original school. Reports indicated great success with this tactic, and the transferred students showed reduced bullying behaviors in their new schools.

room techniques is not necessary. Good teachers know their students best and are best qualified to review curriculum materials and adapt them where necessary to their students' needs. Nevertheless, it's a good idea to meet with classroom teachers (by levels) and to briefly go through the Teacher Manuals, after giving them a chance to review them in advance.

As mentioned earlier in this manual (see page 14), each level of the curricula is designed to help students:

- define and understand what is and what is not bullying

- better understand bullying and its effects

- develop empathy for the victims of bullying

- learn when and how to report bullying

- discover the school's consequences for engaging in bullying behavior

The Kindergarten and First Grade level of the program requires eight sessions to accomplish the above objectives. All other levels of the program require only six.

Each teacher will need a copy of the manual geared to his or her level and will also need access to materials required for presenting the sessions. If possible, have extra copies of the manuals available for other staff members to review, so that they are cognizant of what is going on in the classroom.

As director of *The No-Bullying Program*, either you will serve—or you will need to find someone else to serve—as a resource person for the classroom teachers and as a liaison between teachers, administration, and other school staff regarding materials, access to space, procedural concerns, and the like.

Step 7

Measuring the effectiveness of the program. It is important for you to decide, in advance of implementing the program, how you will measure its effectiveness. You might look at the number of incidence reports your school has of bullying and related behaviors. Consider doing a pre/post tabulation of these reports. It is important to consider that you would expect to have an increase of reports after initiating *The No-Bullying Program*. Like any effective awareness program, reports should increase for a few weeks and then start to go back down. Once that has occurred, an overall decline should result.

Chapter 7: Family Matters

Once you have initiated *The No-Bullying Program* in your school, and you begin to apply consequences to bullying behaviors, you should understand some important principles about meeting with the parents of students who have bullied and with parents of their victims.

First of all, never meet with the parents of a student who bullies and the parents of a student who is a victim at the same time. This invariably intensifies the situation, since parents naturally will defend and advocate for their own child. Each set of parents needs and deserves a separate meeting time, because each set has a separate problem that needs addressing.

Second, no matter how much documentation you may have regarding a child's bullying behavior, his or her parents are more likely to regard their child as the victim. Again, parents normally will defend their child and try to place the blame for bullying elsewhere—for example, on the victim, on the school, on society, even on themselves.

Third, with regard to the parents of children who bully, refuse to argue about "blame" for the behavior. Instead, simply restate the school's commitment to non-violence and its policy/strategy regarding bullying and the consequences for engaging in it.

Fourth, help the parents of children who bully feel that you are there to support them in helping their child experience school as a place where learning is key, respect is essential, and appropriate behavior has its rewards. Make it clear to these parents that, like them, you seek only what is best for their child.

Fifth, parents of children who are victims of bullying may need help in letting go of their feelings of anger or their desire for retribution toward the student who has bullied their child. Again, try to steer parents away from blaming. At the same time, assure these parents that the school is absolutely committed to ending their child's victimization and to making him or her feel that the school is a safe and caring environment.

Sixth, helping parents of children who are victims of bullying recognize and understand the characteristics of victims of bullying (see page 11 of this manual) can empower them to join with the school in helping their child avoid being victimized in the future.

Chapter 8: All-School Kick-Off Assembly

Ending bullying in a school is a serious endeavor. However, it should not be a somber one. Those who worked in developing and piloting *The No-Bullying Program* discovered that holding an up-beat, All-School Kick-Off Assembly was precisely the right move in getting the program off the ground and in gaining student support. Thus, we strongly urge you to plan an All-School Kick-Off Assembly as a sort of pep rally for school safety.

Do as much as you can to publicize the event. Post copies of the No-Bullying Logo Poster (see Appendix, page 37), create banners, send out announcements, invite parents and community leaders. Consider having the school band play.

It is very effective if each adult in the school wears a specially designed *No-Bullying* tee shirt to the kick-off assembly. It shows real solidarity among the entire staff and serves as a visual reminder to everyone that the program merits serious group effort. Tee shirts, stickers, and posters are available through the Johnson Institute and should be ordered well in advance of the kick-off assembly.

Have the school principal introduce and close the assembly. The principal needs to convey a sense of real excitement about *The No-Bullying Program* and the opportunity everyone has to make the school a place where everyone feels safe and likes to be. The principal must then make the following points clear to the students:

1. He or she and every other school staff member wholeheartedly support the program.

2. The program will give students and staff new and important information about bullying that will benefit them all.

3. The program *will* be successful and everyone will work together to make it a success.

4. As a result, the school will be a safer and happier place for everyone.

Consider a number of other speakers to briefly address (two or three minutes) the assembly. You can find speakers from:

- professional agencies that deal with domestic abuse to offer support for victims

- the community leadership, such as the mayor, council person, or other official, to explain how bullying can lead to greater violence and greater problems

- the PTA or parent advisory group to share how critically important it is to parents that schools are safe for their children and to offer their help and support

- student leadership groups to encourage broad support and to act as models of non-bullying

- individual students to read poems or other short pieces pertinent to the topic

Besides "The Enabling Checklist" and the "Sample Letter to Parents," The Appendix of this manual includes a number of visual aids. You may wish to duplicate these aids as handouts or overhead transparencies as you present the All-School Kick-Off Assembly:

- No-Bullying Logo Poster

- No-Bullying Logos

- Definition of Bullying

- Characteristics of Bullies

- Characteristics of Passive Victims

- Characteristics of Provocative Victims

- Bullying Behavior Chart

You may also consider employing these aids when you provide staff training, meet with community leaders, or conduct orientation for parents.

Finally, you may also wish to make posters or handouts that detail your school's "Strategy Statement/Policy" regarding bullying (see pages 16–17), the "Procedure for Reporting Bullying" (see page 23), and the "Consequences for Bullying" you have agreed on (see pages 24–25).

If you decide to offer No-Bullying Tee shirts, ready-made posters, and stickers for sale at your Kick-Off Assembly, plan to have a special table set up to display the items. You may want to order quantities of Tee shirts in assorted sizes ahead of time or else provide an opportunity later on for students to order them through their teacher. As mentioned earlier, however, having a Tee shirt available for each adult to wear during the Kick-Off Assembly is very effective in showing students that the adults are united in their efforts to take action against bullying in your school.

The effort you put into this All-School Kick-Off Assembly will not go unrewarded. It will reap immediate benefits by helping students "buy in" to *The No-Bullying Program* and getting it off to a solid and enthusiastic start.

CONCLUSION

At the beginning of this manual we stated that *The No-Bullying Program* was based on the recognition that everyone deserves a great childhood without violence. But, in fact, perhaps much more than childhood is at stake. *The No-Bullying Program* recognizes that what happens to our children today determines what will happen to all of us tomorrow. Those who bully, who abuse power today, will continue to abuse it in the future. Those who take unfair advantage of the less powerful over and over again will grow to be unstoppable in their abuse, whether that bullying is in the form of an assault and battery or a savings and loan scam. What seems to be at stake, then, is more than a childhood without violence, but an adulthood, a middle-age, and an old-age for us all.

APPENDIX

Enabling Checklist

Sample Letter to Parents

No-Bullying Logo Poster

No-Bullying Logos

Definition of Bullying

Characteristics of Bullies

Characteristics of Passive Victims

Characteristics of Provocative Victims

Bullying Behavior Chart

Enabling Checklist

	Sometimes	Never
1. When I see acts of violence among students, I don't report it.	❑	❑
2. I've gradually lowered my expectations for acceptable student performance.	❑	❑
3. I tend to oversimplify problem behaviors in students who use violence.	❑	❑
4. I view students who bully others as "bad kids."	❑	❑
5. I feel angry, tense, or anxious about having to deal with violence problems in school.	❑	❑
6. I place the blame for students' bullying somewhere other than on the students themselves.	❑	❑
7. I hesitate to involve others when dealing with bullying students because I feel that they or the situation will be mishandled.	❑	❑
8. I don't take action with students who bully others because I fear that the victim will be mistreated again.	❑	❑
9. I wait for students' violent behavior problems to change by themselves.	❑	❑
10. I feel that many of the behaviors described as "bullying" are just normal behaviors for children and adolescents—part of growing up.	❑	❑
11. As long as no one is physically hurt, I look the other way when I see students name-calling, teasing, using put-downs, or provoking others.	❑	❑
12. I avoid dealing with bullying students out of fear for my personal safety.	❑	❑
13. I make excuses for, cover up, or defend certain students involved in bullying or other violence.	❑	❑
14. I avoid places in the school where I know students tend to bully others.	❑	❑

	Sometimes	Never
15. I have ignored the violent or bullying behaviors of staff.	❏	❏
16. I have allowed students to avoid the consequences of their bullying behavior to protect their academic or athletic status.	❏	❏
17. I believe the best course for victims of bullying is to fight back.	❏	❏
18. I believe the best cure for those who bully is to have stronger students give them a taste of their own medicine.	❏	❏
19. I've used violent language or actions while dealing with students.	❏	❏
20. I fail to admit the extent of bullying and other problems with violence in order to protect the school's image.	❏	❏

Dear Parent(s)/Guardian(s):

We know you want the best for your child. We know that you want the school environment to be safe and free of violence. That's why we at [name of school] are beginning a new program called *The No-Bullying Program* to deal with the problem of bully violence in our school. We want to make our school a violence-free and bully-free zone.

As part of *The No-Bullying Program*, your child will be involved in a series of lessons designed to help him or her:

- define and understand what is and what is not bullying

- better understand bullying and its effects

- develop empathy for the victims of bullying

- learn when and how to report bullying

- discover the school's consequences for engaging in bullying behavior

As a school, we have developed a new policy regarding bullying. Under that policy, bullying will not be tolerated, adults will intervene to stop it and apply swift, severe, and consistent consequences to those who engage in bullying behaviors.

The overall aim of *The No-Bullying Program* is not to punish students who engage in bullying. Rather, its primary objective is to shift the balance of power away from those who bully by empowering other students and adults in the school to confront them with their unacceptable behaviors.

Since *The No-Bullying Program* takes a system-wide approach to ending bullying in school, it not only involves the students and school personnel, it involves you, the parents and family. To succeed, the program needs your input.

Please mark your calendar now to join with us on [date] at [place] to learn more about *The No-Bullying Program*. Your support will greatly contribute to our efforts in making [name of school] safer and more nurturing for all our students.

Sincerely,

[name of school principal]

Bullying Happens...

when someone with *more* power

unfairly hurts someone

with *less* power

over and over again.

Power may be:

- physical strength
- social skill
- verbal ability
- or another resource

Kids who bully...

- are excited by their bullying behavior.

- enjoy feelings of power and control.

- lack compassion and empathy for their victims.

- enjoy causing pain.

- are calm and show little emotion.

- blame the victims.

- think that the innocent remarks or actions of others are meant to hurt them.

- are usually average students.

- do not have low self-esteem.

- usually have a small network of friends.

- are successful at hiding their bullying behavior.

- are excited by their victims' reactions such as fighting back.

- who are boys more often use physical force, insults, and threats.

- who are girls more often rely on social alienation and intimidation, such as excluding their victims, threatening them, or making them feel as if they don't belong.

Kids who are passive victims...

- show a lot of emotion.

- rarely tell about being bullied, because they think it will make matters worse, and they don't think adults can help.

- often carry weapons for protection.

- do not encourage attack; they don't "ask for it."

- are sensitive, cry easily, and are easy to pick on.

- may be shy and lacking in social skills.

- are usually insecure and lacking in self-esteem.

- are usually chosen last or left out.

- may appear to lack humor.

- have few or no friends.

- are often anxious and easily upset.

- are bullied repeatedly.

- may use money or toys (as bribes) for protection.

Kids who are provocative victims...

- are pesky and repeatedly irritate others.

- are quick-tempered and prone to fight back.

- get others charged up.

- may be clumsy, immature, restless.

- provoke bullying; they "egg on" kids who bully.

- sometimes look as if they are bullies themselves, but, unlike true bullies, they always lose in the end.

Bullying Behavior Chart

LEVELS	Physical Harm to another's body or property		Emotional Harm to another's self-esteem		Social Harm to another's group acceptance	
	verbal	non-verbal	verbal	non-verbal	verbal	non-verbal
1	Taunting Expressing physical superiority	Making threatening gestures Defacing property Pushing/shoving Taking small items from others	Insulting remarks Calling names Teasing about possessions, clothes	Giving dirty looks Holding nose or other insulting gestures Saying someone has germs or is unclean	Gossiping Starting/spreading rumors Teasing publicly about clothes, looks, etc…	Passively not including in group Playing mean tricks
2	Threatening physical harm Blaming victim	Damaging property Stealing Initiating fights Scratching Tripping or causing a fall Assaulting	Insulting family Harassing with phone calls Insulting intelligence, athletic ability, etc…	Defacing school work Falsifying school work Defacing personal property, clothing, etc…	Insulting race, gender Increasing gossip/rumors Undermining other relationships	Making someone look foolish Excluding from the group
3	Making repeated and/or graphic threats Practicing extortion Making threats to secure silence: "If you tell, I will…"	Destroying property Setting fires Biting Physical cruelty Making repeated, violent threats Assaulting with a weapon	Frightening with phone calls Challenging in public	Ostracizing Destroying personal property or clothing	Threatening total group exclusion	Arranging public humiliation Total group rejection/ostracizing

Bullying involves exploitation of a less powerful person. There must be an unfair advantage being exerted. Bully/victim conflict is best understood as a dynamic relationship. Whether or not a behavior is bullying depends on its effect upon the victim. This chart was designed to assist with the identification of bullying behavior in situations where an unfair advantage exists. The seriousness for all levels of behavior should be evaluated based on the harm to the victim and the frequency of the occurrences.

Additional Resources

The following materials are available from the Johnson Institute. Call us at 800-231-5165 for ordering information, current prices, or a complete listing of Johnson Institute resources.

No-Bullying Program Materials

T-shirts with the No-Bullying Logo displayed on the front, posters, stickers, and extra teaching manuals for your school may be ordered simply by calling the sales department at Johnson Institute.

Video Programs

An Attitude Adjustment for Ramie. 15 minutes. Order #V429

Anger: Handle It Before It Handles You. 15 minutes. Order #V450

Broken Toy. 30 minutes. Order #V462

Choices & Consequences. 33 minutes. Order #V400

Conflict: Think About It, Talk About It, Try to Work It Out. 15 minutes. Order #V451

Dealing with Anger: A Violence Prevention Program for African-American Youth. 52 minutes (males), 68 minutes (females). Order #V433 (for males); Order #V456 (for females)

Double Bind. 15 minutes. Order #V430

Good Intentions, Bad Results. 30 minutes. Order #V440

It's Not Okay to Bully. 15 minutes. Order #5883JH

Peer Mediation: Conflict Resolution in Schools. 28 minutes. Order #V458Kit

Respect & Protect: A Solution to Stopping Violence in Schools and Communities. 28 minutes. Order #V460

Tulip Doesn't Feel Safe. 12 minutes. Order #V438

Publications

Bosch, Carl W. *Bully on the Bus.* Order #P413

Boyd, Lizi. *Bailey the Big Bully.* Order #P422

Carlson, Nancy. *Loudmouth George and the Sixth Grade Bully.* Order #P414

Crary, Elizabeth. *I Can't Wait.* Order #P431

————. *I'm Furious.* Order #P506

————. *I'm Mad.* Order #P509

————. *I Want It.* Order #P427

————. *My Name Is Not Dummy.* Order #P429

Cummings, Carol. *I'm Always in Trouble.* Order #P418

————. *Sticks and Stones.* Order #P420

————. *Tattlin' Madeline.* Order #P421

————. *Win, Win Day.* Order #P419

Davis, Diane. *Working with Children from Violent Homes: Ideas and Techniques.* Order #P244

DeMarco, John. *Peer Helping Skills Program for Training Peer Helpers and Peer Tutors.* Order #P320Kit

Estes, Eleanor. *The Hundred Dresses.* Order #P411

Fleming, Martin. *Conducting Support Groups for Students Affected by Chemical Dependence: A Guide for Educators and Other Professionals.* Order #P020

Freeman, Shelley MacKay. *From Peer Pressure to Peer Support: Alcohol and other Drug Prevention Through Group Process.* Order #P147-7-8 (for grades 7, 8); Order #P147-9-10 (for grades 9, 10); Order #P147-11-12 (for grades 11, 12)

Garbarino, James, et al. *Children in Danger.* Order #P330

Goldstein, Arnold P., et al. *Aggression Replacement Training: A Comprehensive Intervention for Aggressive Youth.* Order #P329

Haven, Kendall. *Getting Along.* Order #P412

Johnsen, Karen. *The Trouble with Secrets.* Order #P425

Johnson Institute's No-Bullying Program for Grades K–Middle School. Order #546Kit

Julik, Edie. *Sailing Through the Storm to the Ocean of Peace.* Order #P437

Lawson, Ann. *Kids & Gangs: What Parents and Educators Need to Know.* Order #P322

Mills, Lauren. *The Rag Coat.* Order #P417

Moe, Jerry, and Peter Ways, M.D. *Conducting Support Groups for Elementary Children K–6.* Order #P123

Olofsdotter, Marie. *Frej the Fearless.* Order #P438

Perry, Kate, and Charlotte Firmin. *Being Bullied.* Order #P416

Peterson, Julie, and Rebecca Janke. *Peacemaker® Program.* Order #P447

Potter-Effron, Ron. *How to Control Your Anger (Before It Controls You): A Guide for Teenagers.* Order #P277

Remboldt, Carole. *Solving Violence Problems in Your School: Why a Systematic Approach Is Necessary.* Order #P336

———. *Violence in Schools: The Enabling Factor.* Order #P337

Remboldt, Carole, and Richard Zimman. *Respect & Protect®: A Practical Step-By-Step Violence Prevention and Intervention Program for Schools and Communities.* Order #P404

Sanders, Mark. *Preventing Gang Violence in Your School.* Order #P403

Saunders, Carol Silverman. *Safe at School: Awareness and Action for Parents of Kids in Grades K–12.* Order #P340

Schaefer, Dick. *Choices & Consequences: What to Do When a Teenager Uses Alcohol/Drugs.* Order #P096

Schmidt, Teresa. *Anger Management and Violence Prevention: A Group Activities Manual for Middle and High School Students.* Order #P278

———. *Changing Families: A Group Activities Manual for Middle and High School Students.* Order #P317

———. *Daniel the Dinosaur Learns to Stand Tall Against Bullies. A Group Activities Manual to Teach K–6 Children How to Handle Other Children's Aggressive Behavior.* Order #P559

———. *Trevor and Tiffany, the Tyrannosaurus Twins, Learn to Stop Bullying. A Group Activities Manual to Teach K–6 Children How to Replace Aggressive Behavior with Assertive Behavior.* Order #P558

Schmidt, Teresa, and Thelma Spencer. *Della the Dinosaur Talks About Violence and Anger Management.* Order #P161

Schott, Sue. *Everyone Can Be Your Friend.* Order #P435

Stine, Megan, and H. William Stine. *How I Survived 5th Grade.* Mahwah, NJ:Troll Associates, 1992. Order #P415

Vernon, Ann. *Thinking, Feeling, Behaving.* (for grades 1–6) Order #P250

Villaume, Philip G., and R. Michael Foley. *Teachers at Risk: Crisis in the Classroom.* Order #P401

Wilmes, David. *Parenting for Prevention: How to Raise a Child to Say No to Alcohol/Drugs.* Order #P071

———. *Parenting for Prevention: A Parent Education Curriculum—Raising a Child to Say No to Alcohol and Other Drugs.* Order #PO72T

ORDER FORM

BILL TO:

Name _____

Address _____

_____

City _____ State _____ Zip _____

ATTENTION: _____

Daytime Phone: (   ) _____

PURCHASE ORDER NO. _____

❑ Individual Order   ❑ Group or Organization Order

If Ordering for a Group or Organization:

Group Name _____

SHIP TO: (if different from BILL TO)

Name _____

Address _____

_____

City _____ State _____ Zip _____

ATTENTION: _____

Daytime Phone: (   ) _____

TAX EXEMPT NO. _____

Please send me a free copy(ies) of Johnson Institute's:	❑ ___ Publications and Films Catalog(s) ❑ ___ Training Calendar(s) ❑ *Observer*, a quarterly newsletter

PLEASE SEND ME:

QTY.	ORDER NO.	TITLE	PRICE EACH	TOTAL COST

For film/video titles, please specify: ❑ 1/2" VHS   ❑ 3/4" U-Matic   ❑ 1/2" Beta   ❑ 16mm

SHIPPING AND HANDLING		
Order Amount	**U.S.**	**Outside U.S.**
$0–25.00	$ 6.50	$8.00
$25.01–60.00	$ 8.50	$10.00
$60.01–130.00	$10.50	$13.50
$130.01–200.00	$13.25	$19.50
$200.01–300.00	$16.00	$24.00
$300.01–over	8%	14%

Please add $8.00 ($10.50 Canada) for any videotapes ordered.

OFFICE USE ONLY

Order No. _____

Customer No. _____

QVS, Inc.

❑ Payment enclosed
❑ Bill me
❑ Bill my credit card:

❑ MasterCard
❑ VISA
❑ American Express
❑ Discover

Expiration Date: _____

Signature on card: _____

Total Order _____
(Orders under $75.00 must be prepaid)

6.5% Sales Tax _____
(Minnesota Residents Only)

Shipping and Handling _____
(See Chart)

TOTAL _____

Have you ordered from the Johnson Institute before? **Yes** ❑   **No** ❑

If yes, how?   **Mail** ❑   **Phone** ❑

JOHNSON INSTITUTE®

7205 Ohms Lane ❖ Minneapolis, Minnesota 55439-2159
(612) 831-1630 or toll-free: 1-800-231-5165